THE GREATEST RECORDS IN SPORTS
RACING'S
GREATEST RECORDS

Heather Moore Niver

PowerKiDS
press.

New York

Published in 2015 by The Rosen Publishing Group, Inc.
29 East 21st Street, New York, NY 10010

First Edition

Editor: Katie Kawa
Book Design: Reann Nye

Photo Credits: Cover (track) Gunnar Assmy/Shutterstock.com; cover (Patrick) Jamie Squire/NASCAR/ Getty Images; cover (Busch) Jerry Markland/Getty Images Sport/Getty Images; p. 5 (top) Archive Holdings Inc./Archive Photos/Getty Images; p. 5 (bottom) Chris Trotman/ Getty Images Sport/Getty Images; p. 7 Rainer W. Schlegelmilch/Getty Images; p. 8 Bob Harmeyer/ Archive Photos/Getty Images; p. 9 Robert Laberge/Getty Images Sport/Getty Images; p. 10 Gary Newkirk/Getty Images Sport/Getty Images; p. 11 John Biever/Sports Illustrated/Getty Images; p. 13 Focus On Sport/Getty Images; p. 15 (top) Grey Villet/The LIFE Picture Collection/Getty Images; p. 15 (bottom) Brian Lawdermilk/Getty Images Sport/Getty Images; p. 17 (top) Andy Lyons/ Getty Images Sport/Getty Images; p. 17 (bottom) Jamie Squire/Getty Images Sport/Getty Images; p. 19 (Petty) John Harrelson/Getty Images Sport/Getty Images; p. 19 (Daytona) Bill Frakes/ Sports Illustrated/Getty Images; pp. 21, 23, 29 (Patrick) Jared C. Tilton/Getty Images; p. 25 Jonathan Ferrey/Getty Images Sport/Getty Images; p. 26 RacingOne/ISC Archives/ Getty Images; p. 27 Rick Lewis/Shutterstock.com; p. 29 (car) Matt Sullivan/NASCAR/Getty Images; p. 30 Education Images/Universal Images Group/Getty Images.

Library of Congress Cataloging-in-Publication Data

Niver, Heather Moore.
Racing's greatest records / by Heather Moore Niver.
p. cm. — (The greatest records in sports)
Includes index.
ISBN 978-1-4994-0234-6 (pbk.)
ISBN 978-1-4994-0182-0 (6-pack)
ISBN 978-1-4994-0229-2 (library binding)
1. Automobile racing — Juvenile literature. 2. Automobile racing — History — Juvenile literature. I. Niver, Heather Moore. II. Title.
GV1029.N58 2015
796.72—d23

Manufactured in the United States of America

CPSIA Compliance Information: Batch #CW15PK: For Further Information contact Rosen Publishing, New York, New York at 1-800-237-9932

CONTENTS

Automobile racing (often shortened to "auto racing") is an exciting and fast-paced sport featuring speedy cars and talented drivers. Race cars of all kinds speed around **circuits** and down roads all over the world. The first races were in the 1880s, and the first official race took place in France in 1894. Another race took place in Chicago, Illinois, the next year. This race marked the beginning of organized auto racing in the United States.

Different kinds of auto racing feature different cars and tracks. Each kind of racing has its own records held by the sport's best drivers. Records are determined by comparing **statistics**, which are also called "stats." Many racing stats measure how fast race cars can go, while others show which drivers have won the most races.

DIFFERENT KINDS OF RACING

Some popular kinds of auto racing include drag racing, midget-car racing, and rally racing. This book will focus on two of the most famous kinds of racing in the United States: IndyCar racing, which is a form of open-wheel racing, and NASCAR, which grew out of stock-car racing.

Auto racing has changed a lot since its earliest days!

The fastest race cars in the world are open-wheel cars. They only have one seat and have wheels that stick out beyond the body of the car. Most cars have wheels under their body. Open-wheel cars can reach speeds of over 200 miles (322 km) per hour!

In 1906, the first Grand Prix race was held in France. "Grand Prix" once meant the best race in a country. Now, it refers to open-wheel races that count towards the Formula 1 (F1) Drivers' World Championship. In F1 races, open-wheel cars follow very detailed rules, or formulas, for how their cars are put together and how they drive. The top 10 drivers in each Grand Prix earn points toward the championship.

SUPERIOR STATS
CAREER GRAND PRIX WINS

DRIVER	COUNTRY	WINS
MICHAEL SCHUMACHER	GERMANY	91
ALAIN PROST	FRANCE	51
AYRTON SENNA	BRAZIL	41
SEBASTIAN VETTEL*	GERMANY	39
FERNANDO ALONSO*	SPAIN	32

* = active driver

Michael Schumacher won five F1 championships in a row, from 2000 to 2004.

MICHAEL SCHUMACHER (1969–)

Michael Schumacher started racing when he was a kid. He won his first F1 race in 1992. In 1994, he won the first of his seven F1 championships. That's the record for most championships in the history of F1 racing. Schumacher also won a record-breaking 91 Grand Prix races!

One of the most famous open-wheel races is the Indianapolis 500, which is also known as the Indy 500. It began in Indianapolis, Indiana, in 1911. This 500-mile (805 km) race happens on the Indianapolis Motor Speedway. At first, the track was **paved** with rock and tar. Before long, though, it was repaved with brick and nicknamed "The Brickyard." Today, it's covered with **asphalt**, but there's still a 36-inch (91 cm) section of brick on the track. This section marks where the race begins and ends, because the track is a circuit.

Many drivers have won the Indy 500 more than once, but only three have won four times. A.J. Foyt, Rick Mears, and Al Unser are all tied for that record.

A.J. FOYT
(1935–)

A.J. Foyt's nickname, "Super Tex," came from his hometown of Houston, Texas. Foyt is one of the best drivers in the history of the Indy 500. In addition to being tied for the most Indy 500 wins, he holds the record for most Indy 500 starts in a row (35).

Open-wheel race cars in the United States are sometimes called Indy cars because they're used in the Indy 500. This style of racing is also known as IndyCar racing for the same reason.

SUPERIOR STATS
FOUR-TIME INDY 500 WINNERS

DRIVER	YEARS WON
A.J. FOYT	1961, 1964, 1967, 1977
AL UNSER	1970, 1971, 1978, 1987
RICK MEARS	1979, 1984, 1988, 1991

The Indy 500 track isn't actually 500 miles long. Racers drive around a track that's 2.5 miles (4 km) long until they've driven 500 miles. One time around the track is called a lap. It takes 200 laps to reach 500 miles. In 1996, Eddie Cheever Jr. set the record for the fastest single Indy 500 lap at 236.103 miles (379.971 km) per hour.

Al Unser holds the record for most Indy 500 laps led in his career, with 644. In 2013, Tony Kanaan broke the record for the fastest average winning lap speed at 187.433 miles (301.644 km) per hour. Speed records are broken often, as new **technology** helps people create faster race cars nearly every year.

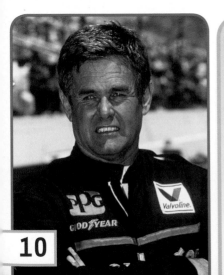

AL UNSER
(1939–)

Besides holding the record for most laps led, Al Unser is also the oldest Indy 500 winner. In 1987, Unser was almost 48 years old when he raced across the finish line, breaking the record his brother Bobby held at the time. The win was Unser's record-tying fourth Indy 500 victory.

Al Unser's son, Al Unser Jr., is also a race-car driver. He won the Indy 500 twice.

SUPERIOR STATS
FASTEST INDY 500 LAP
(AS OF 2014)

DRIVER	YEAR	LAP SPEED (IN MILES PER HOUR)
EDDIE CHEEVER JR.	1996	236.103
TONY KANAAN*	2003	229.188
MICHAEL ANDRETTI	1992	229.118
TONY KANAAN*	2005	228.102
JUSTIN WILSON*	2013	226.940

* = active driver

POLE POSITION

Each Indy 500 race features 33 cars. The fastest qualifying driver gets to be in the pole position, or the best position on the track. The pole position is commonly on the inside of the front row. The driver in the pole position doesn't have to pass other cars to get to the front.

Where drivers start in the Indy 500 depends on three races. First, the 33 cars do four full laps in a qualifying race. The fastest nine drivers advance to a second race: the Fast Nine Shootout. The driver with the fastest average time in these races wins the pole position. Drivers who finished the first qualifying race in positions 10 through 33 race again to determine their starting positions.

RICK MEARS
(1951–)

Rick Mears was the youngest of the four-time Indy 500 winners, earning all four of his victories before he turned 40. Mears holds many Indy 500 records, including most pole-position starts. He's also the only driver to win from the pole position in three different decades.

The driver in the pole position is called the "pole sitter." Rick Mears was the Indy 500 pole sitter more times than anyone else in the race's history.

SUPERIOR STATS
MOST TIMES IN INDY 500 POLE POSITION

DRIVER	POLE POSITIONS	YEARS
RICK MEARS	6	1979, 1982, 1986, 1988, 1989, 1991
REX MAYS	4	1935, 1936, 1940, 1948
A.J. FOYT	4	1965, 1969, 1974, 1975
HÉLIO CASTRONEVES*	4	2003, 2007, 2009, 2010

* = active driver

Early racing stock cars looked like ordinary cars, but had been modified, or changed, to make them faster. Modern racing "stock cars" look like ordinary cars outside, but inside, they've been built for racing. In 1939, organized stock-car racing began in Langhorne, Pennsylvania. In 1947, the National Association for Stock Car Auto Racing (NASCAR) was formed in Daytona Beach, Florida. By the 1970s, NASCAR had helped stock-car racing gain popularity, and several other stock-car racing organizations were created, too.

Stock cars usually race on an oval, paved track. NASCAR even has its own **premier series** of 36 races called the Sprint Cup Series, also known as the Sprint Cup or Cup Series.

ILLEGAL BEGINNINGS

Stock-car racing began during Prohibition in the United States, which took place from 1919 to 1933. During this time, it was illegal to sell **alcohol**. People who made and sold it illegally needed fast cars to outrun the police. For fun, the drivers would challenge each other to races. After Prohibition ended, people still raced these fast cars for fun.

Stock-car racing has grown to become one of the most popular sports in the United States.

To win the NASCAR Sprint Cup Championship, drivers have to perform well in all 36 races. Every driver wins points based on their finishes in the first 26 races. Then, the 10 drivers with the most points compete in a final series of 10 races called the "Chase for the NASCAR Sprint Cup." Points don't carry over from the first 26 races, and the winner of the Chase wins the Cup Championship.

Dale Earnhardt and Richard Petty share the record for most Cup Championships, with seven. Richard "The King" Petty earned his nickname by being the most successful NASCAR driver of all time. He won 200 Cup Series races in his career, which is the most any driver has ever won.

SUPERIOR STATS
MOST CAREER CUP CHAMPIONSHIPS

DRIVER	CHAMPIONSHIPS	YEARS
RICHARD PETTY	7	1964, 1967, 1971, 1972, 1974, 1975, 1979
DALE EARNHARDT	7	1980, 1986, 1987, 1990, 1991, 1993, 1994

While Richard Petty is known as "The King," Dale Earnhardt was called "The Intimidator" because he was such a feared and fearless driver. He wasn't afraid to bump other cars or cause spinouts on the track.

DALE EARNHARDT
(1951–2001)

Dale Earnhardt was one of the most popular drivers in NASCAR history. He won 76 Cup Series races during his career, which was cut short when he was killed in a crash on the track. His son, Dale Earnhardt Jr., followed in his father's footsteps and is also a successful NASCAR driver.

17

If you're looking for the most famous NASCAR race in the United States, look no further than the Daytona 500. Every February since 1959, drivers and their fans have gathered for this race at the Daytona International Speedway in Daytona Beach, Florida. Stock cars speed around a track that's 2.5 miles (4 km) long. They race around it 200 times, just like open-wheel cars do in the Indy 500.

Lee Petty won the first Daytona 500. He's Richard Petty's father! Richard Petty holds the record for most Daytona 500 wins, with seven.

SUPERIOR STATS
MOST DAYTONA 500 WINS

DRIVER	WINS	YEARS
RICHARD PETTY	7	1964, 1966, 1971, 1973, 1974, 1979, 1981
CALE YARBOROUGH	4	1968, 1977, 1983, 1984
BOBBY ALLISON	3	1978, 1982, 1988
DALE JARRETT	3	1993, 1996, 2000
JEFF GORDON*	3	1997, 1999, 2005

* = active driver

Races such as the Daytona 500 can be **dangerous** and even deadly. The crash that killed Dale Earnhardt took place at the 2001 Daytona 500.

RICHARD PETTY
(1937–)

Richard Petty might have racing talent in his blood, since his own father won the first Daytona 500. Petty holds many NASCAR records, including the most Daytona 500 wins. He retired from racing in 1992, and he was **inducted** into the NASCAR Hall of Fame in 2010.

The stock cars in the Daytona 500 go very fast, but generally not as fast as Indy cars. Buddy Baker set the record for the fastest Daytona 500 winning speed in 1980 when he raced along the speedway at an average of 177.602 miles (285.823 km) per hour. In 1964, Richard Petty set the record for most laps led in one Daytona 500 race, with 184. He's also known for his record of 780 total laps led in his career.

At the end of the Daytona 500, the winner is given a **trophy** called the Harley J. Earl Trophy. Trophies are not just awarded to the winning driver. The winning crew and team owner are also recognized for their part in helping the driver win.

BUDDY BAKER
(1941–)

Buddy Baker is considered by many to be the fastest of NASCAR's most famous drivers. During a race in 1970, Baker became the first driver to reach speeds of over 200 miles (322 km) per hour on a closed course.

The Daytona 500 is sometimes called the "Great American Race."

SUPERIOR STATS
FASTEST DAYTONA 500 WINNERS

DRIVER	YEAR	AVERAGE SPEED (IN MILES PER HOUR)
BUDDY BAKER	1980	177.602
BILL ELLIOTT	1987	176.263
DALE EARNHARDT	1998	172.712
BILL ELLIOTT	1985	172.265
RICHARD PETTY	1981	169.651

Before fans pack the stands to watch the Daytona 500, there are two weeks of races called Speed Weeks. They include pickup-truck races and sports-car races, as well as the Daytona 500 qualifying races.

The starting lineup for the Daytona 500 is decided in a different way than other NASCAR races. The pole position and the outside front row position are decided based on qualifying speeds. Then, the remaining 41 spots are decided by how the cars finish in two 125-mile (201 km) races.

The pole position has produced more than a few Daytona 500 winners, such as Jeff Gordon. The record for the most times a driver has been in the Daytona 500 pole position is four. Three drivers—Cale Yarborough, Buddy Baker, and Bill Elliott—are tied for this record.

Kyle Busch and other current racing stars are looking to break the records set by drivers such as Yarborough. Busch already has records for being the youngest driver to win the pole position in a number of NASCAR races.

SUPERIOR STATS
MOST DAYTONA 500
POLE POSITIONS

DRIVER	POLE POSITIONS	YEARS
CALE YARBOROUGH	4	1968, 1970, 1978, 1984
BUDDY BAKER	4	1969, 1973, 1979, 1980
BILL ELLIOTT	4	1985, 1986, 1987, 2001

CALE YARBOROUGH
(1939–)

Cale Yarborough was the first NASCAR driver to win three Cup Championships in a row (from 1976 to 1978). He won the pole position at Dayton four times, which is a record he shares with Buddy Baker and Bill Elliott. Yarborough was inducted into the NASCAR Hall of Fame in 2012.

NASCAR and IndyCar both have teams. Some teams are made up of hundreds of people! The team owner is in charge of everyone. The owner's main job is to get **sponsors** to help pay for the fastest car possible. A team manager helps the owner keep everything running, and a crew chief works with the manager, too, but is focused on building the race car. One team can have multiple drivers on it. This gives the owner more chances to win a race.

SUPERIOR STATS
MOST DAYTONA 500 WINS BY TEAM
(AS OF 2014)

TEAM	OWNER	WINS	YEARS
PETTY ENTERPRISES	RICHARD PETTY	9	1959, 1964, 1966, 1970, 1971, 1973, 1974, 1979, 1981
HENDRICK MOTORSPORTS	RICK HENDRICK	8	1986, 1989, 1997, 1999, 2005, 2006, 2013, 2014
WOOD BROTHERS RACING	GLEN AND LEONARD WOOD	5	1963, 1968, 1972, 1976, 2011

Jeff Gordon

Famous drivers such as Jimmie Johnson, Jeff Gordon, and Dale Earnhardt Jr. have all driven for Hendrick Motorsports.

One of the most successful NASCAR teams is Hendrick Motorsports. As of 2013, this team holds a record of 11 NASCAR Cup Championships. The most successful team at the Daytona 500 was Petty Enterprises, owned by Richard Petty. Petty Enterprises changed its name in 2009 to Richard Petty Motorsports.

RICK HENDRICK
(1949–)

Rick Hendrick was born in North Carolina. He started Hendrick Motorsports in 1984. Hendrick has won **awards** like NASCAR's Bill France Award of Excellence. His teams have won a Cup race every season since 1986, which is the longest current **streak** in NASCAR.

Women have raced their way into the record books, too. It's becoming more common to see female drivers in major races. However, they've had to fight to be respected by other drivers and fans since the sport's earliest days. Janet Guthrie became the first woman to finish the Indy 500 in 1977. She helped pave the way for other female drivers with her success. In 1978, Guthrie finished in ninth place in the Indy 500.

Danica Patrick is one current driver working hard to prove that women can drive just as well as men. Patrick led the pack for 19 laps in her first Indy 500 race. This was the first time a woman had led a lap in the Indy 500.

JANET GUTHRIE

JANET GUTHRIE
(1938–)

Janet Guthrie became the first woman to qualify for the Indy 500 in 1977, but she wasn't able to finish the race. However, she finished the next year's race in ninth place, even with a broken wrist! Guthrie also qualified for the 1979 Indy 500.

Patrick began her racing career as an IndyCar driver.

SUPERIOR STATS
BEST FEMALE INDY 500 DRIVERS

DRIVER	HIGHEST CAREER FINISHING POSITION
DANICA PATRICK	3 (2009)
JANET GUTHRIE	9 (1978)
LYN ST. JAMES	11 (1992)
SIMONA DE SILVESTRO	14 (2010)
SARAH FISHER	17 (2009)

NASCAR has a long history of including women in racing. In 1949, Sara Christian became the first woman to race in a NASCAR premiere series event when she drove in the Strictly Stock race at Charlotte Speedway. Two weeks later, Christian and her husband became the only married couple to ever compete in a NASCAR Cup Series race.

Janet Guthrie was also a NASCAR driver. In 1977, she became not only the first woman to start in the Indy 500, but also the first woman to start in the Daytona 500. Danica Patrick followed in Guthrie's footsteps and hit the NASCAR tracks in 2010. She became the first woman to lead a lap of the Daytona 500 in 2013. Patrick finished eighth in that race, which is the best finish ever by a woman in the Daytona 500.

Danica Patrick has been known to say that she was raised to be the fastest driver — not just the fastest woman — on the track.

DANICA PATRICK
(1982–)

Danica Patrick is one of the most famous drivers — male or female — in auto racing today. On the way to her record-setting finish in the 2013 Daytona 500, Patrick became the first woman to qualify for the pole position in the Great American Race.

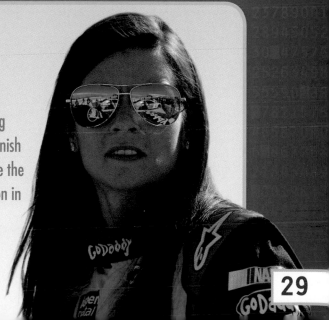

NO FINISH LINE IN SIGHT

Whether it's a race known all around the world, such as the Indianapolis 500, or a smaller race on a dirt track, watching drivers race to the finish line is always exciting! All kinds of races are held all around the world. With each race, drivers chase the records set by the sport's most famous and talented stars.

As technology improves, the cars will change and the speeds on the track will be faster. It seems there's no finish line in sight for the thrilling world of auto racing!